MY *Teacher* BELIEVES *in Me!*

The Educator's Guide to At-Promise Students

DR. VICTOR RIOS
DR. REBECA MIRELES-RIOS

Five Rivers Press

ISBN: 9781722600013

Table of Contents

Acknowledgements

OVER TWENTY YEARS AGO in 1998, a group of at-promise students at a middle school set us up on our first date. Rebeca was a student teacher working on her teaching credential and Victor was a counselor at the school site. We worked together to find solutions for students who were involved in drug use, fighting, gangs, and delinquency. While we both thought fondly of each other, we were committed to remaining professional. However, the students saw something between us before we ever did. They approached Rebeca and asked her if she would go on a date with Victor. Then they approached Victor and asked him the same. One day, we both decided to appease the students and go on a "lunch date" across the street from the school at a Chinese restaurant. During that meal we realized there was a deeper connection. We agreed to go out on a dinner date...and the rest is history; we have been married twenty years, we have three kids (two of them are now adults and attend four-year universities), we have supported each other through our careers, and continue to work together to improve the lives of at-promise students.

We want to give thanks to each other for being there through thick and thin and for remaining committed to one another and to our joint purpose, despite the various adversities we have faced. We also want to thank those at-promise students that set us up on our first date.

Finally, we want to thank our three children Maya, Marina, and Marco, who have been our greatest teachers when it comes to parenting. We love you. Keep living the legacy.

CHAPTER 1

The Role of Emotional Support and Cultural Responsiveness in Supporting At-Promise Students

"I'm not sayin' I'm gonna change the world, but I guarantee that I will spark the brain that will."
—TUPAC SHAKUR

EDUCATORS FACE THE COMPLICATED TASK of reaching, motivating, and retaining "at-risk" students in school. Despite the importance of supporting such students, the reality is that educators have countless students to work with and often do not have the amount of time or resources necessary to truly support these "at-risk" students. As a consequence, these students are failed by the education system, and subsequently become more vulnerable to negative life outcomes. Desiring a community that would make them feel accepted and valued, they might turn to the streets to develop a sense of belonging, self-worth, and dignity in order to survive. Very often the streets provide a false sense of protection and belonging when all other institutions, such as schools and social programs, have failed. Pursuing survival strategies also exposes these youth to police contact, harassment, brutality, and incarceration. These young people who come from marginalized backgrounds are too often pushed out of the educational system and into the streets or the juvenile system.

Many researchers and educators have referred to this "funneling through" as the "school-to-prison pipeline." One of the core ideas of the "school-to-prison" pipeline is that students from disadvantaged backgrounds are often criminalized and turn to a life of criminality due to the discrimination and lack of support they receive at school. Because of the necessity to engage in certain behaviors in order to survive, some of these students overlook the long-term impacts of crime and its consequences, which can have repercussions on their development and life-course trajectories.

When thinking about how to best support these students, it is important to ask ourselves, how can we as educators shift the educational system's understanding of marginalized youth from a deficit perspective to an asset perspective? How can we provide them the opportunities they deserve, and acknowledge the potential they have to succeed? Rather than labeling students from underprivileged backgrounds as "at-risk" youth who will inevitably fail in the educational system, they should instead be regarded as "at-promise" students that already possess the tools necessary to succeed in school, but just need affirmation, support, resources, and assistance to utilize those tools. From this point forward, we refer to these students as **"at-promise."** An at-promise person is someone who encounters adversity but has the inner capacity to overcome this adversity. This definition assumes that almost every individual facing adversity is able to overcome these odds, if provided with the right recipe of support.

Authority figures can easily misunderstand young people's intentions, especially if these students have not learned the proper communication skills to express themselves. Some may possess a lens that perceives these youth as violent, gangbanging thugs who are uninterested in an education and conventional success—an "at-risk" perspective. Instead, let's see them as "at-promise" students, helping each of them to find their internal potential. Labels have powerful effects on actions. Young people who are labeled as "at-risk" will inevitably see doors close before them. What does society do with risks? We often reject them, exclude them, and even incarcerate them. This subgroup of students who have left school are not dropouts, but pushouts—individuals whom schools had intentionally or unintentionally left behind, rejected, or discouraged from moving forward in their educational trajectories.

Another important practice to engage in when attempting to transform the lives of disadvantaged students is ***cultural responsiveness***. This term has been used in relation to how one designs his or her lessons, as it is sometimes termed, "culturally responsive" pedagogy, where one's teaching recognizes students' cultural backgrounds. Designing such lessons is important and has greatly proven to promote student engagement, leading to higher academic achievement. Moreover, caring is also a key element in being culturally responsive. Showing care for students in their own cultural context allows educators to support them in a meaningful manner. Angela Valenzuela (2010) refers to this as ***authentic caring***. A teacher's ability to empower students is not only an academic endeavor—it is also an emotional job: teachers should allow students to feel valued and affirmed for their authentic selves and potential, not just for the grades they can achieve. This book encourages teachers to connect with their students through what we term, ***Emotion-Informed Approaches*** in the educational process. Emotion-informed approaches are different from trauma-informed approaches in that they account for the full complexity of human emotion. Marginalized students are not just "traumatized." They are also cheerful, vibrant, happy, empathetic, and optimistic. These emotional states have to be accounted for and utilized as part and parcel of the transformation process. When we learn how to tap into our students' cultural and emotional worlds, we become transformative educators. Another difference between emotion-informed approaches and trauma-informed approaches is our assessment of the systemic, community, and school contexts that operate simultaneously to impact the lives of marginalized students. At-promise students do not spontaneously land in their situations, but rather an entire social world of neglect and victimization has led them there. Students' stories become central in understanding this process. A transformative teacher knows that, over time, with the right kind of guidance and resources, marginalized students become masters of their own destinies and learn how to advocate for themselves and their communities. An emotion-informed framework allows the educator to connect with students, first and foremost, at an emotional level, in order to tap into the academic and self-empowerment assets that students possess.

The first principle in emotion-informed approaches is understanding and showing respect for your students' community, culture, background, and family. How do the communities that your students come from show love, care, and compassion? How can we replicate these practices and truly embrace our students? This knowledge can help tear down walls that young people build around themselves as a defense mechanism. The following three strategies are fundamental for beginning the process of emotion-informed approaches and culturally responsive pedagogy in educational settings:

1. **REMOVE THE DEFICIT PERSPECTIVE IN EDUCATION**
   Rather than solely thinking of students as individuals who have to be taught to become good test takers or well-behaved citizens, teachers should also encourage students to be comfortable with sharing their life stories and adversities; their experiences should be used to empower them in their developmental trajectory. Transformative teachers must treat these youth as students with immense potential, rather than students who are destined to fail because of their

circumstances. The goal is to frame their life struggles as a source of confidence, strength, and empowerment, rather than shame, weakness, and vulnerability.

2. VALUE THE STORIES THAT STUDENTS BRING TO YOUR CLASSROOM

Many students have overcome seemingly insurmountable odds that reflect the power, grit, character, and resilience they possess. As educators, encourage students to frame their stories and experiences as sources of strength that have molded them into the person they are today. Help these students refine their stories and be proud of whom they are, by welcoming their families, cultures, communities, and skill sets that they have acquired while grappling with life's complexities. Even in a math class, a subject with very little time to discuss personal circumstances, a teacher can open up the class with a "high and low" activity. What was your high for the week, what was your low for the week? They can all respond in a written note to the teacher. Then some can share with the class. This activity takes no more than 10-15 minutes and allows the teacher to make an emotional connection with students, helping them feel included and listened to. And now, back to our math lesson: $72x - 40 = 176$, solve for x.

3. PROVIDE STUDENTS WITH THE TOOLS THEY NEED FOR SUCCESS

Identifying "grit" and strength alone is not sufficient for helping young people thrive. Students must also be provided adequate resources, such as counseling, mentoring, financial opportunities, and educators who have undergone proper emotional-support training. Such resources can prove to be effective for reaching disadvantaged students by providing them with the tools which will allow them to learn and grow from their mistakes, rather than simply being reprimanded by pulling them out of class, ostracizing them, and employing other disciplinary actions that cause students to feel detached and abandoned rather than supported. Transformative justice is the process by which educational institutions reflect on their own actions towards students and improve their capacity for reintegrative positive approaches to working with conflict and disciplinary challenges. Transformative justice is an approach to discipline and community building that allows students to take ownership of their behavior and reflect on how their environment has shaped their understanding of how to react in certain situations. One example of transformative justice is when a student is caught plagiarizing or cheating: the school provides the student a context to understand why this is wrong, how this affects other students, and how this interrupts their own learning trajectory. The student can be provided with an opportunity to develop a lesson plan to teach other students about plagiarism and its effects on the learning process. The student might also be given the role of conducting a research project on why students cheat, and on how the educational system, and specifically standardized testing, often creates pressures on students to do well by any means necessary, and how this may create a culture of plagiarism and cheating. Solutions may be presented by the student for how to improve our education system and reduce these pressures. In this case, rather than ejecting the student from the learning process, they have become an important contributor and have also "learned their lesson" in a more reintegrative and productive manner.

In order to switch the focus of students' stories from victims to survivors who are able to overcome adversity, students need the support of caring adults who can help them reframe their stories by recognizing their potential and assets. Because young people spend much of their waking hours in the classroom, it is crucial for educators to take on this role and provide nurturing relationships that are aimed at helping these students thrive and reach their potential. Providing this viable support system to your students could enhance and promote a more positive, productive identity of themselves.

To make the education system more empowering for our most vulnerable students, *all* educators must work towards an unwavering understanding of at-promise students. We must not give up on them because of their unique circumstances and difficulties in school. Instead, we must help these students "refine" their stories by identifying the grit, resilience, and character they have developed through their life experiences. Once these students refine their life stories and harness their experiences as a source of strength rather than weakness, they have increased capacity for improving their academic performance. Teachers must believe in their students and shift the way they perceive them from "at-risk" to "at-promise," and from being a "threat" to an "asset." In order to best endorse academic success for our students, they must be valued for whom they are and where they come from, and have their individual needs supported as a contribution to the classroom community.

ACTIVITY: A TEACHER'S ADVERSITY

Directions: Think about your childhood experiences and how they impacted you as a student.

- Think back to an adversity you have faced in life. In what ways have your experiences helped define you?
- Have they helped you build grit, resilience, and character, and in what ways are they being applied in your life today?
- Was there a mentor, teacher, counselor, or other caring adult in your life who helped you to believe in yourself?

Use the space below to share your thoughts.

CHAPTER 2

A Teacher's Purpose: The Key To Transformative Education

"Great teachers empathize with children, respect them, and believe that each one has something special that can be built upon."

—ANN LIEBERMAN

PEOPLE DECIDE TO BECOME EDUCATORS for many different reasons. Some are inspired by a positive encounter with a teacher, while others may choose to teach because they had a negative academic experience and are motivated to change the system. Others decide to enter the field simply because they enjoy the subject they teach. Some teach because they want to save lives and change the world. Regardless of what it is, everyone has a purpose for entering into the teaching profession. Why did you become an educator? What is your purpose for working with students?

In one of his YouTube videos, Comedian Michael Jr. reminds us, "When you know your why, your 'what' becomes more impactful because you're walking towards your purpose." When you realize, acknowledge, remember, and embrace your purpose as an educator, you are able to fully reflect your sense of purpose onto your students. Students have the ability to recognize teachers who are purposeful not only in their delivery of lessons, but also in how they engage with students. Your purpose for teaching can influence the impact you make on your students' lives.

As a teacher, you might spend over eight hours a day, five days a week, nine months a year with students. Understanding your reason for teaching will help you be intentional in how you take on your role as a teacher and become a good steward of the responsibility that you have chosen to commit to. It will aid in your approach to being culturally responsive, offering emotional support, and valuing what your students bring to your classroom. Is teaching "just a job," or is it something you truly enjoy and is intrinsically significant to you? As educators, you have the power to transform the lives of young people every day, thus it is important to be reminded about the "why" behind your "what."

A purpose comes from the heart. It is what drives human action. Some people's purpose is to make money, work with wildlife, or cure illnesses. However, as an educator, you entered this profession with the intent of educating students. What led you here? And more importantly, how can you remind yourself on a consistent basis to think back to your purpose?

When a student is not engaging and is frustrating you, one strategy can be to reminisce on your own experiences as a student and the kind of obstacles that prevented you from engaging in class. One teacher shared her experience about an interaction with a student in her 10th grade math class who was assigned to complete a worksheet for extra credit. This student decided to play games on his phone instead of doing the assignment. The teacher asked him to put his phone away and work on the assignment, but the student said, "No, I don't want to do it." Rather than yelling at him, or sending him to the principal, the teacher asked him, "Why don't you want to complete the assignment?"

He responded, "I don't want to do the extra credit assignment because I am already satisfied with my grade." The teacher went on to explain how important extra credit points can be at the end of the school year to help improve a grade that may be reduced because of an upcoming test or other future assignment: "It's like a savings account; you don't know what can happen in the future, and you can use the extra credit points in an emergency when you need it to help boost your grade." At that moment, the student quickly picked up his pencil and completed the assignment. Reflecting on her own experiences in school when she was not given an explanation for the assignments she was asked to complete, this teacher vowed that in her career as an educator, she would answer questions and connect with her students in ways that would aid their learning and promote their engagement with the class.

In other cases, educators report having developed their purpose for teaching from negative experiences in their own educational process. Consider the case of Rebeca, one of the authors of this book. When Rebeca was in 6th grade, she was voted the ugliest girl in school by her classmates. With hurt feelings, Rebeca looked to her teacher in hopes that her teacher would stand up on her behalf, but instead, her teacher laughed along with the rest of the students. While the teacher may not have intentionally hurt Rebeca's feelings, Rebeca was heartbroken and traumatized by the experience. On that day, Rebeca told herself, "I will become a teacher one day so that if this happens to another student, I can be there to care for and protect them." Rebeca eventually received her teaching credential from UC Berkeley and taught 6th grade for over seven years until she became an education researcher and professor. Rebeca's purpose as an educator came from her own experience as a student, when she did not feel cared for by her teacher. A teacher's purpose is a powerful transformative tool. It helps us remember why we became educators to begin with, and allows us to form strong connections with our students.

ACTIVITY: WHAT IS YOUR PURPOSE FOR WORKING WITH STUDENTS?

Directions: Take a moment to think about why you decided to become an educator. Was there an experience you had as a student that led you to this field? If so, what was it? Was the experience positive or negative? How does it influence your purpose for being an educator? When you are clear with your purpose, you have the power to transform lives as an educator. Below are some examples to help you get started!

- A positive or negative experience as a student
- Wanting to help students in need
- The money!

CHAPTER 3

From At-Risk to At-Promise: Removing the Deficit Perspective in Education and Recognizing Students' Potential

"My teacher believed in me so much, she tricked me into believing in myself."
— DR. VICTOR RIOS

IMAGINE YOURSELF AS A STUDENT and the following is your day-to-day routine:

Although most students in your school set their alarms for around 7:00 AM, you wake up at 5:30 AM because you have to make breakfast for your younger siblings and help get them ready for school because your single mother leaves for work at 5:30 AM. Your first class begins at 8:15 AM, but the bus stop for the bus you take to school is located one mile away from where you live and includes frequent stops along the way—the entire ride is over 90 minutes. You arrive just a few minutes late, but when you attempt to explain to your teacher that you had to help your siblings and that the bus was delayed, he or she quickly dismisses your explanation, and marks you "tardy." You feel unheard and unsupported.

As you sit in class, you feel exhausted from watching your younger siblings last night while your mom worked her second job closing shift at the diner, and realize your homework from yesterday is not complete. When you try to communicate to your teacher why your homework is incomplete, again, they quickly dismiss you and deduct points from your assignment, with no opportunity of receiving an extension or making up the points. Again, you feel unheard, uncared for, and dismissed.

When your teacher begins the lesson and starts writing on the whiteboard, you are unable to see the words because you have been struggling to see clearly the last couple weeks. You don't realize it because your family can't afford an optometry visit, but you desperately need glasses. You raise your hand to ask to sit closer, but your teacher tells you not to interrupt her while she is talking, and to wait to ask her questions. But you cannot see at all. When you are finally allowed to ask questions, the bell rings and it is time to walk to the next class. You hurry up from your seat, because you already feel behind and don't want to receive another tardy.

While walking through the hallways, another student approaches you with unkind remarks about the way you are dressed. He comments on your fatherless status, calling you a "bastard." He knows your father has not been in your life since you were a toddler. You grow frustrated and angered, and do your best to move on with your day, despite thinking about how you will probably never see your father again.

After the last bell, you run to the bus stop to make sure you are home in time to watch your siblings while your mother is still at work. As much as you want to catch up with schoolwork, you cannot stay for after school tutoring. Your teachers tell you, "Well if you really wanted to improve your grades, you would stay after school for tutoring."

Stories like these are realities for many young students. Some face even more severe obstacles and challenges in their daily lives. Students as young as 10-years-old with experiences like these are often perceived as "troublemakers," "a lost cause," "drop-outs," "gang members," "thugs," "delinquents," and "criminals." They are blamed and punished for their life circumstances that are beyond their control, and are often pushed out of the educational system because of a lack of understanding between themselves and their school faculty. As educators, it is important do away with these negative assumptions and labels and instead consider the assets that these students do in fact possess and can bring to the education system. The way the educational system labels and treats young students has significant consequences for their well-being and development. Therefore, it is crucial that we move beyond describing the behaviors of marginalized young people in ways that divide, misrepresent, and deny the full range of their humanity, and that treat these young people with stigma, disrepute, and punishment. When we change our perception, together, we can change the way we perceive young people from being "at-risk" to "at-promise." In April of 2019 the State of California passed a bill, AB 413, changing the label of "at-risk" to "at-promise" in educational code, policy, and practice. For years, Victor Rios and other education reformers have advocated for this change. In his 2011 book, *Punished: Policing the Lives of Black and Latino Boys,* Victor wrote: "At-promise youth are those youth who have traditionally been labeled "at-risk"—youth who have been marginalized, have marginalized themselves, or both. An issue with labeling young people as "risks" is that this may generate the very stigma that I am analyzing in this study. Therefore, I am calling them what many community workers call them: at-promise." By 2019 Victor and other advocates had convinced school districts to change the way they labeled at-promise young people. The state legislator picked up on this momentum and made the motion to eliminate "at-risk" from the law:

THE PEOPLE OF THE STATE OF CALIFORNIA DO ENACT AS FOLLOWS:

AB 413, as amended, Jones-Sawyer. Education: at-promise youth. Existing law uses the terms term "at-risk" and "high-risk" to describe youth for purposes of various provisions of the Education Code. and Penal Codes. This bill would delete the term "at-risk" and "high-risk" and would replace those terms it with the terms term "at-promise" and "high-promise" for purposes of these provisions. The bill would, *for purposes of the Education Code,* define "at-promise" and "high-promise" to have the same meanings meaning as "at-risk" and "high-risk," respectively. Existing law defines and refers to specified young people with the presence of certain risk factors that make them more likely to be involved with criminal street gangs or the criminal justice system as "at-risk youth." This bill would change the references in statute to these individuals from "at-risk youth" to "at-promise youth."

When working with educators, Victor tells them, "My teacher believed in me so much, she tricked me into believing in myself." Let's practice believing in all students regardless of how they have been labeled. The following scenarios contain vignettes of students. For each scenario, change the student's narrative, making it an asset-based perspective (e.g. what potential does the student have?). When we believe in students and their potential, it often provides them with a blueprint for transformation and academic success.

STUDENT #1	Disaffected, distracted, wears large t-shirts, baggy pants, falls asleep in class, and works after school helping parents with their food truck business until closing every night.
ASSUMPTION	"He's a slacker, a gang member, and falls asleep in class because he does not care about school. He will not graduate high school."
CHANGED NARRATIVE	"____ ____ ____ ____ ____ ____ ____ ____ ______________________________________."

STUDENT #2	Attention deficit, poor test scores, behavioral problems, social with peers, and volunteers at local animal shelter.
ASSUMPTION	"A class clown who will never be able to succeed."
CHANGED NARRATIVE	"____ ____ ____ ____ ____ ____ ____ ____ ____."

STUDENT #3	Colorful stickers on notebooks and textbooks, does not like using pencils and instead chooses to complete assignments using colorful pens, has large handwriting, is a cheerleader, wants to get married at eighteen, and enjoys babysitting.
ASSUMPTION	"She is a dumb cheerleader who does not take school seriously and will end up pregnant soon."
CHANGED NARRATIVE	"______________________________ ______________________________ ______________________________ ______________________________ ______________________________ ______________________________ ______________________________ ______________________________ ______________________________."

CHAPTER 4

Teacher-Student Relationships: Cultivating Meaningful Connections Between Teachers and Students

"I don't teach subjects, I teach students."
—MS. FLORA RUSS

THE ILLUSTRATION OF ONE STUDENT'S DAILY ROUTINE in the previous chapter is just one example of what many students experience. How can we make students who experience countless adversities feel a sense of relief, connection, and support at school? According to Dr. James Comer, professor of Child Psychiatry at Yale University, a good school culture can provide positive relationships and sense of belonging, which in turn gives students comfort, confidence, competence, and motivation to learn. (Comer, 2005). Specifically, the teacher-student relationship is important for both social and academic outcomes. When students feel they belong and are safe and secure in their learning environments, they develop the opportunity to learn and grow. Thus, connecting with your students and demonstrating your support can give life to their motivation to learn: this begins with being intentional in the way that you interact with your students.

As teachers, students perceive you as authority figures. They view you as "the one in charge of class," and the "one in power." Many of the students admire you and yearn for your recognition, acceptance, and appreciation. Imagine yourself being recognized or affirmed by your Principal or Superintendent. They tell you, "I notice all that hard work and effort you have put into preparing your class for the first day of school." How does that make you feel? Valued? Cared for? Just as it feels great to be validated by your superiors, students hanker for the same treatment from their teachers. Human affirmation is universal; we all need it and we all thrive from it.

Imagine yourself as a student who has had one or more extremely difficult days, but you have a teacher who shows kindness, concern, and genuine interest in how you are doing every day you enter into their classroom. How might that make you feel? Perhaps you are surprised that someone actually takes an interest in who you are as a whole person rather than simply as a pupil whose test scores reflect the skill of their teacher. Would this stable and caring interaction motivate you to show up to class? Would it encourage you to put your best effort into your schoolwork?

When teachers feel they are unable to relate to some of their students, they may also feel hesitation and confusion on how and when to show encouragement and support; they may not know how to go about asking questions that would convey their interest in their students. And frankly, oftentimes teachers are less likely to connect with students from another culture or race. This means that educators should strive to become "racially literate." We refer to ***racial literacy*** as *the process by which individuals become aware of the history and struggles of the various racial and cultural populations they educate.* If we are teaching a Jewish student, shouldn't we make an effort to learn about their holidays and traditions? The same efforts should be made with all students—it is important to inform oneself and garner understanding of students' diverse cultures and races. How might a Latinx student with immigrant parents be taught to relate to authority figures? Do they look authority figures in the eyes when they have a conversation, or is this a sign of disrespect? It is important for us to know these social rules in order to avert conflict with our students, as we may assume they are being disrespectful in times when they are simply following the social and cultural rules they have learned in other contexts.

What about a LGBTQ+ student? How might we learn to be reflexive about their experiences and struggles? We welcome you to think about developing what we refer to as "intersectional literacy." ***Intersectional literacy*** *is the process by which individuals are constantly seeking to understand, learn about, and empathize with the various identities and multiple situated standpoints and contexts that fellow human beings live and experience.* Learning about sexuality, gender, class, race, ability (as opposed to disability), and the religious struggles our students' experience is crucial in the journey of providing them emotional support. Legal scholar Kimberlé Crenshaw (1989) introduced the idea of "intersectionality" to describe the various experiences, characteristics, and oppressions that individuals face based on the multiple identities and categories that define them. This idea motivated us to develop the concept of intersectional literacy and to apply it to everyday practice and human interaction in a diverse society. The more we all learn to reflect on how others are "othered" by the many categories that define them, and recognize our own privilege in relation to this othering, the more we are able to support those who have been left behind.

Imagine teaching a Black-female-lesbian student from a low-income household. What are the unique struggles that accompany each of the identities she lives with? How can we acknowledge each of these struggles and support her whole person? By having these conversations and answering these questions about our students, we come a step closer to achieving intersectional literacy.

To understand our students and the various worlds they come from, the reality is that there are no "perfect questions" to be asked at the "right time." It is a matter of having the proper perspective that will allow you to ask the "right" kind of questions. It is important to keep in mind that when your students feel acknowledged, heard, and understood, this can have monumental consequences on their learning and self-perception. Ask yourself, "What would I ask my own child or a relative of mine during a special holiday?" You are likely imagining questions such as "How was your weekend? What sports have you watched lately? Are there any movies you have enjoyed watching? Why?" Apply this same responsiveness to your students when interacting with them. While it may take time for your students to receive your support, as many of them may not be used to being treated in such a kind way, it is crucial to have patience and not give up on students because they do not immediately respond to your efforts. Trying to understand where they come from and seeing their potential will slowly break down the psychological walls they've built to protect themselves.

When students receive support from a trusted adult like yourself, it can not only improve your students' academic performance, but also their general development as a person. A study by Woolley and Grogan-Kaylor (2006) found that receiving support from authority figures is a strong predictor of school-appropriate behavior, positive attitudes, and academic performance. While providing support to your students can positively impact the way they learn, it can also influence who they are as individuals outside of the classroom and the decisions they make.

Now, imagine being affirmed by a significant person in your life, not for accomplishing anything specific, but rather for simply being you. How does *that* make you feel? Coined by psychologist Carl Rogers, *unconditional positive regard* is support and encouragement given with "no strings attached;" it is not taken away when one makes a mistake or fails a test. Unconditional positive regard gives a person the freedom to learn and try new things without the fear of having their status as "being worthy" withdrawn from them. Today's educational system tends to define students' academic status, and consequently their "worth" as a student, by using test scores and letter grades; this can be compared to *conditional positive regard,* which is defined as "positive regard, praise, and approval, that depends upon the child" (McLeod, 2014). In other words, how the child behaves or performs academically are factors that will either earn or undermine positive regard (McLeod, 2014). In contrast, unconditional positive regard allows students to feel cared for and valued in spite of their shortcomings and mistakes—their sense of being "worthy" as a person is not contingent upon their behavior and accomplishments in school (Benson, 2016). However, unconditional positive regard is not simply providing students with trophies for doing nothing, or just calling students "brilliant." We are talking about telling students, "You matter," "I am here for you," "I believe in you," "You got this!"

Some students come from a home where their parents provide conditional positive regard, which leads them to believe that their worth as a person needs to be earned rather than given freely. This mindset can go on to impact other aspects of their lives, such as their choices when choosing a major, career, college, etc.—these students may feel that they do not deserve certain things. Providing unconditional positive regard has the power to change how young people see themselves: worthy, regardless of how many accolades they receive.

Victor, one of the authors of this book, had a high school teacher, Ms. Russ, who completely reversed his life trajectory. She would always tell her colleagues, **"I don't teach subjects, I teach students."** What she meant by this was that her purpose for becoming an educator was to help students become their best possible selves, and not just to stand in front of a class and repeat everything she had learned about a given subject. Unconditional positive regard is not about telling a student, either explicitly or implicitly, that they are only a good student if they are able to pass a test or perform well. Instead, it is about bestowing unwarranted respect and value upon another person; it is about imparting worth in someone without tying this worth to memorizing, passing a test, or completing a difficult assignment. Not only will providing unconditional positive regard allow students to feel valued and cared for, but it will also develop a positive environment where these students can discover, acknowledge, and freely express their immense potential.

ACTIVITY HOW WAS POSITIVE REGARD EXPRESSED TO YOU?

Directions: Think back to freshman year of high school. Did you ever have a teacher who affirmed you? How did that make you feel? Share the specific strategy they used to support you. If you did not have a teacher who affirmed you, please reflect on what you would have loved for one of your teachers to do for you when you were starting your high school career.

CHAPTER 5

Educator Projected Self-Actualization: How to Shape Students' Future Selves

"If we can share our story with someone who responds with empathy and understanding, shame can't survive."
—BRENÉ BROWN

WE DEFINE ***Educator-Projected Self-Actualization*** as *the process by which an educator believes in a student and shows them the path to a successful future—a future that the student has yet to imagine—providing a powerful practical guide for this student and allowing him or her to discover new life changing possibilities.* Educators can project a better, brighter future for their students on a daily basis by recognizing their strengths and communicating how they can use these strengths to succeed. When an educator projects for a brighter future for students, they embrace and pursue this projection, leading to a higher chance of accomplishment.

Educator-Projected Self-Actualization begins with encouraging a person to become their best self by utilizing his or her own capabilities and strategies, rather than the inflexible rules and regulations that institutions have established and strictly enforced. When a person fully realizes and acknowledges his or her wide range of talents and potentialities, this person is considered to be **self-actualized**, a concept made prominent by the psychologist Abraham Maslow. Self-actualization can be achieved when one is able to discover, accept, and express their full potential. Seeking self-actualization helps people develop the motivation necessary to fulfill their potential to the highest degree. Psychologist Carl Rogers proposed that self-actualization can only be achieved when a students' ideal self (whom he or she would like to become) overlaps with his or her actual self (his or her real behavior and personality). People who are not able to attain self-actualization are likely to be less happy and content with their lives than those who have. In the context of education, if students perceive themselves as incapable of succeeding in a particular subject, or "not good enough," they will be hindered from realizing the full capacity of their potential and consequently reaching self-actualization, which can lead to significant mental conflict and strife. This is where you, the teacher, come in: the more you encourage students by conveying that you believe in them, the more likely you are to convince them to believe in themselves.

Unconditional positive regard plays an important role in Educator-Projected Self-Actualization; when someone is met with unconditional positive regard, it can help them develop a strong sense of self-worth and self-discovery, which are linked with self-actualization. If a student is bestowed with unconditional positive regard from an authority figure, it can enable them to feel that they have a purpose, by which they are then motivated to pursue. As an educator, it is important that you believe your students have valuable contributions to provide in your classroom, school campus, and community. As their teacher, you already exist within a "continuum of care" in each of their lives; you are one of the people in their lives who is expected to provide them with love and positive emotional support. The "continuum of care" is a system of support in which all parties take responsibility for supporting student well-being. The institutions involved can be eclectic: schools, families, churches, non-profits, law enforcement, social services, etc. The key in creating a continuum of care is that all parties are on the same page in terms of how to treat, engage with, and support students. One party cannot be punitive while the other party is restorative. All parties have to engage in conversation to come up with a systematic plan for how adults within these systems will engage with students. Transformative justice is one example of an approach that all parties can engage in. When a police officer stops a student on the street during school hours, his goal could be to figure out how to best support the student and coordinate with teachers and counselors with a common plan on how to re-engage this student with school. Below is an example of one continuum of care. What other parties can be included in this model?

The Continuum of Care

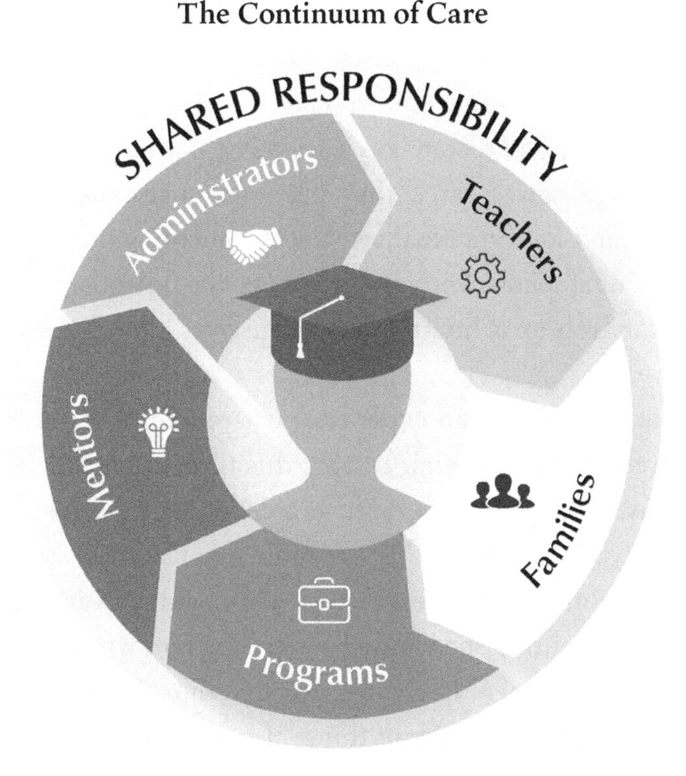

Research has consistently demonstrated that emotional support becomes a universal denominator in positive academic experiences and trajectories. When emotional support and unconditional positive regard are provided across institutional settings as part of the continuum of care, we see healthy kids develop and thrive both inside and outside of the classroom. Although you may have students who are not yet open to receiving your support, and may also even strongly reject it, when they are ready one day, and you are there for them, that perfect match will transform lives.

You have the opportunity every day, five days a week, to influence how students perceive themselves. You are given the chance to project to your students a future that they cannot yet imagine for themselves. In many instances, students might not have time to form dreams because their focus is solely on trying to survive their everyday lives—they are dealing with scenarios like trying to manage school while also helping their family pay the bills. Maybe some students are not able to dream simply because they have not been given a reason to. They may have a social environment that makes it seem like it is not possible for them to go to college, enter a career they love, or even be a successful student in school. Envisioning a life they want is something that may be of far reach to your students. Verbally expressing the potential your students possess can transform how they see themselves and what they are able to achieve.

Victor himself had an experience where a teacher acknowledged and expressed his potential. During this time in his life, Victor had gone to juvenile hall and was seen as a delinquent (see his book *Street Life: Poverty, Gangs, and a Ph.D.* for more details on his story), but his teacher Ms. Russ nevertheless provided him with unwavering support and assured him that she would be there for him when he was ready to make a commitment to change. She told him, "Victor, I know that one day you will do important things. I know one day you will meet presidents." Although he did not initially believe in his own potential, she "tricked him into believing it." Ms. Russ saw the assets that the one-day-to-be Dr. Rios possessed, and she didn't allow them to slip by and go unnoticed. She did not see Victor as the "thug" that others saw him as. She saw him as a future professional capable of making change in this world. She made it known by verbally expressing his potential to him and encouraging him to utilize his capabilities for success. Twenty years later, Victor had the opportunity to travel to the White House and advise the Obama Administration on policing and gun violence in the US. He even met President Barack Obama. Victor was holding his four-year-old son Marco in his arms when President Obama walked up to him. President Obama looked at Marco, raised his open hand in front of him and said, "Give me five, don't leave me hanging." In that moment Victor thought of his teacher. He thought to himself, "Ms. Russ, how did you know?" While Ms. Russ was not a fortune-teller, she was an incredible teacher who made a commitment to project for her students a future that they had not even begun to imagine.

Your belief in your students' abilities directly influences their own perception of their potential for success. Think about the concept of a self-fulfilling prophecy: If teachers regard their students as full of potential and capabilities, the students will see this in themselves and act accordingly. On the other hand, if students are treated as if they are destined for failure, then they will internalize this treatment, believe it themselves, and consequently act that way. Let's reverse the negative effects of the self-fulfilling prophecy when educators do not believe in their students. Even if your students do not yet see their own potential, trick them into believing in themselves!

ACTIVITY: THE POWERFUL IMPACT OF BELIEVING IN YOUR STUDENTS
Describe a time in your life when someone believed in you when you did not believe in yourself. Did this person help you see your own potential? How did they help you cultivate your potential?

CHAPTER 6

Understanding Social Location: Another Step in Being Culturally Responsive

"When we have kids in our life, they are other people's children, too, and we have to give them the very best that we have."

—LISA DELPIT

THE KEY TO BUILDING CONNECTIONS with our students is understanding where they come from and knowing their social location. Social location can be defined as the places and experiences that our students' lives are built upon. Social location is a person's physical environment and sense of place. It is important for us to understand the various factors that make up a student's social location, such as their neighborhood, family, culture, race, gender, social class, age, identity, ability, religion, and sexuality. Recognizing our students' social location is consequential because it influences the way they see the world, and in turn the way they interact with their school environment. By understanding students' social location, and our own, we take a step towards becoming culturally responsive. As educators, it is important to be culturally responsive when getting to know who your students are and respecting the communities they come from; being culturally responsive can help students use their own experiences to empower themselves in their educational experiences and in their life trajectory thereafter.

One way to be culturally responsive and recognize students' social locations can be to provide an equitable learning environment by encouraging students to express meaning in a variety of ways. Today's educational system has a rigid approach to attaining successful learning in the classroom, however, learning in different ways ought to be something that is welcomed and valued. Not every student can learn in the same way, and some students understand certain strategies better than others. Thus, making space to allow each student to bring their own unique experiences into the classroom will empower them to translate those experiences into their own style of learning. Being able to incorporate their stories of adversity and resilience into their academic experience allows students to ground themselves in their school environment. When students feel that their teachers understand them and know where they are coming from, they are more likely to want to learn and be engaged in the classroom.

When Victor's teacher Ms. Russ attempted to help him return to school and prepare for college, she asked him to share his story with her. Despite being his computer science teacher, a course with little room to share one's story as part of the curriculum, Ms. Russ understood that in order to *teach* her students, she had to first *reach* her students. Before Victor would learn how to program computers, Ms. Russ had to first get him to develop an interest in the class. This is when she invited him to her class during lunch one day and told him,

> I know you are very private, but I also know you have gone through a lot in life. Maybe you are not into school at this moment, but I want you to know that when you are ready to change your life around I will be here for you. I don't expect

you to share much Victor, but tell me something, what is one thing about your family that makes you proud?

At first Victor remained quiet, thinking that he had nothing to share about his family. "We are just a bunch of broke people with no education," he thought to himself. But then he thought about his uncle Ruben, who had served as a father figure for Victor when he grew up without a father. Victor smiled and told Ms. Russ, "I got this uncle."

"You have this uncle that makes you proud of who your family is. Why?" She responded.

"Because, I go to work with him each morning at 4 A.M. before going to school."

Victor and his uncle would collect glass bottles that often left his body scraped and his clothes bloody from broken bottles. Ms. Russ not only listened to his story, but welcomed it into her classroom, reminding young Victor that his family, culture, and community have taught him a hard-work ethic that can be used to empower himself in the academic world, and which could allow him to later return and empower his community.

"You have a strong family who knows how to help each other and survive." Ms. Russ told Victor. "Why don't you use this opportunity to get an education not just for yourself, but to make your uncle proud and let him know that all his lessons of hard work taught you to work hard at school."

Victor had never thought about school in this way. He always believed the conventional assumptions of the educational system: "Education is for *you* to succeed and obtain a life of prosperity and success for *yourself*."

While Victor dreamed about a good life, more important to him was the idea that he could potentially help his family and community. Ms. Russ understood that Victor came from a familial culture where entire extended families and communities supported each other in survival and prosperity. Why not apply this to education?

When attempting to reach at-promise students, an educator might consider if this student comes from a familial culture, where the value of helping others is sometimes more important than the goal of personal academic and professional success.

Young Victor went on to graduate from high school, undergraduate, and graduate school. Today, he is an award-winning Sociology professor, an Associate Dean of Social Sciences, an author of five Books, and a national speaker. Connecting with your students, being aware of their challenges, and helping them believe in their own potential will ultimately empower students to succeed.

Having insight and understanding of a population that is frequently overlooked by many is crucial for teaching students who come from different backgrounds, especially those from marginalized backgrounds. Immigrant students are one example of marginalized groups who need a specialized sense of understanding and support. Often, the families of low-income immigrant students have chosen to leave everything in their home country behind, in order to start afresh for the benefit of gaining freedom and safety in a completely new one. They work hard to provide for their loved ones to ensure they are well taken care of; most rely on other family members to help them get settled until they are able to financially support themselves. Learning about the challenges that people face and the obstacles they had to overcome in order to live in the United States can give teachers a new perspective of those who have immigrated to this country. The hope is that educators will recognize the efforts and sacrifices these students make to survive in their communities. These very same skills can be translated to academic work, allowing students to be successful in their studies, and in turn foster an environment where "foreigners" are made to feel welcomed and not "foreign" to the classroom, school, or American society. Educators need to assure recently immigrated students that they are capable of contributing to American society and eliminate the "fitting in culturally" definition of academic success.

Ms. Russ is an example of a teacher who took the time to understand her students' social location. She connected with her students and made the effort to understand each of their individual worlds by meeting their families and seeing where they lived. For example, one Sunday afternoon, Ms. Russ drove to a neighborhood that was notorious for violence and abuse, a stark contrast from Ms. Russ's "nice" middle-class neighborhood. But despite the socially-constructed fear that surrounded young Victor's childhood home, Ms. Russ made an effort and took the time to pay a visit to young Victor Rios and his mother. As Victor's mother opened the door, Ms. Russ said "Hola"—one of the few Spanish words that she knew.

"Hello," Victor's mother responded—one of the few English words his mother knew.

Despite the language barrier, Ms. Russ made an effort to talk to his mother, with his little sister's help translating. "Tell your mom your brother is not in trouble," she told his sister. "I am just here to say hello and see how everyone is doing." This short, twenty-minute trip to see her students' families once a semester went a long way. Was Ms. Russ wasting her time by trying to talk to a parent who could not understand her? No, because human connection has no language! Victor's mother received the message that his teacher cared for him and his family and this affirmed her to push Victor to continue with school despite the various family adversities they faced, including not being able to pay the electricity bill at times and being in the dark.

Ms. Russ understood that in order to teach young people who had seemingly given up on school, she had to first earn their respect; she knew she had to gain their permission to teach them. Other teachers had the opposite expectations from students. In response, the students resisted, and, in doing so, a fail-fail classroom environment was created. The teachers failed in being effective educators and the students failed in their academics. The key to success for Ms. Russ was mutual respect; she believed in her students and knew they had to give their consent for her to teach and support them. Ms. Russ understood that it takes human connection to reach students who have been left behind.

As an educator who values learning experiences that draw on students' prior knowledge and history, you can effectively teach students from diverse backgrounds and communities, as well as communicate effectively with their parents and families.

While conducting home visits like Ms. Russ did is not always feasible and sometimes unrealistic, neighborhood walk-throughs are another option. Neighborhood walk throughs can consist of a few educators and community members that gather and visit students' neighborhoods and community. This walk through includes visiting local businesses that students and families frequent: community organizations, houses of worship, and walking by some of the students' homes. You can let students know about this walk through and ask students to provide you a guide of where they play, and also show you where they feel safe and unsafe. Upon reconvening at school, you now have a plethora of discussion topics about the students' neighborhoods, such as local stores, certain streets, parks and other locations where students gather. This understanding brings the educator a step closer to walking in their students' shoes.

ACTIVITY: SOCIAL LOCATION
Directions: List three practices you have engaged in, or can engage in the process of understanding your students' social locations.

Practice #1	
Practice #2	
Practice #3	

CHAPTER 7

Mind, Body, Soul: A Holistic Approach to Education

"To agree to learn from a stranger who does not respect your integrity causes a major loss of self. The only alternative is to not learn and reject the stranger's world."
—HERBERT COLE

MOTIVATING, EDUCATING, AND PREPARING at-promise students for success is an important challenge you are given as an educator. In building relationships with your students, it is important to remember that some of them will not want to open up and will resist and possibly even reject you. Don't take this resistance or rejection personally. Remember that at-promise students are like oysters in the sea; they will open up when they are ready. If you are not there when they are ready, they will clam back up, and shut down. Thus, earning your students' trust is an important step for enabling student learning. Quite often educators will tell us that they have tried and tried, with no avail, to help a student.

"I just had to throw my hands up and focus on the many others that do respond," they tell us.

In response, we tell them that our support for students has to be unconditional, relentless, and consistent. What if at the moment a student opens up and is ready to change their life, they learn we have already turned our backs? They will simply clam back up. We have to let students know we are there for them when they are ready, and show them that warmth, kindness, empathy, and support on a daily basis.

Treating each of your students with dignity, respect, integrity, and most importantly, as human beings with the potential to succeed in school and the workforce, can help them open up and feel confident that you care. Furthermore, engaging with your student as a whole person can help create a culture of success. As an educator working with at-promise students, consider the work you do as a healer. Sometimes our students arrive to our classrooms injured from the various adversities they have faced. Our job is to provide them the right prescription to help them heal. This work of healing the whole person is three-fold: a transformative educator works to heal and strengthen the mind, body, and soul of their student.

Our **MIND, BODY, AND SOUL APPROACH** is a model of healing that teaches young people to care for their multiple manifestations in order to best develop their strengths as individuals:

- Mind—Learning new academic material and academic strategies for developing a deeper understanding of the world and for succeeding in school.

- Body—Engaging in physical activity and team-building activities to develop trust, stay fit, and find positive means for tapping into endorphins, having fun, engaging in healthy social connection, and, developing a good sense of self.

- Soul—Reflecting on one's personal experiences, journaling about them, reframing one's story from victim to survivor, and sharing them with others in order to take control of our own stories and destinies.

Trauma that many young people experience, especially those who come from the harshest conditions, can inflict so much damage on their general well-being, not only in the present, but also well into their adult years. Many youth who have missed school because of unforeseen circumstances within their families, like victimization or health issues, are often told when they return,

> "You have missed too many days; there is nothing we can do for you," or "Why are you still coming to school—you are not going to graduate."

This attitude enables students to see no other option but to stop attending school and venture into the world, feeling uncared for and given up on. Changing our perspective for how we see at-promise students is only the beginning of the process of changing the way we label and treat them. Demonstrating that you believe in your students can in turn strengthen their belief in themselves and their abilities. These students are capable and just need the right connection with mentors, professionals, and educators to inspire them to become the next generation of leaders in their communities.

Although many students have remarkable stories of resiliency and overcoming adversity, some are raised to avoid showing vulnerability and to shun attention. As a result, they become more inclined to bottle up their emotions and memories, rather than seeing adversity as a steppingstone to success, as a light to overcome years of darkness. Students can be taught about the resilient nature of humanity and that anyone has the potential to overcome even the harshest conditions, if caring individuals facilitate the process of healing their minds, bodies, and souls. Educators should teach on the principle that stories of adversity and resilience are powerful. Framing their stories of struggles as stories of overcoming the odds can ignite a transformation and instill a sense of empowerment. Psychologists have documented that when people recount traumatic experiences from a perspective of resiliency rather than victimization, they can change their memories of the events and positively influence their emotions and future trajectories. For example, a person suffering parental abandonment can decide to pursue higher education in order to support a family and be a responsible parent, rather than giving up on their education because of their difficult upbringing. This framework can be used in your own classroom by sharing your own stories of resiliency with your students. This process will help them reframe their stories of victimization, as they recognize the immense strength and grit that exists within the obstacles they have faced and overcome in their lives. You can also urge them to hone in on this grit and expand it to help them reach future positive milestones in life.

While seeing your students through a holistic perspective and working on healing and strengthening their mind, body, and soul will not be the complete solution for helping those who are unengaged or unmotivated, it is nevertheless a step towards the process of changing the way we label and treat disadvantaged young people. Demonstrating that we believe in our students will in turn strengthen their own beliefs in their potential and capabilities. We must be a group of committed individuals working together to achieve a common goal: to show the world that no youth is too at-risk, bad, unmotivated, or unintelligent to do better. Adults who treat youth with dignity and respect, listen to them, are socially aware, and understand the youths' backgrounds can indeed impact young people's lives in incomprehensible ways.

When one hears the term "diversity," it is common to think of it as people who come from various types of backgrounds. While the traditional definition is valued and welcomed in today's school system, there still remains a contradiction between this "valued" and "welcomed" approach and how one actually views students' unique styles of learning. Because it is expected that students abide by the rigid standards of school and learning, they are often discouraged from using their own abilities and methods of learning. In turn, this hinders students from reaching their full potential and accomplishing a task to the best of their ability. Thus, rather than feeling their unique learning style is valued, they are expected to learn how they all "should" learn.

In order to transform student learning and success, listening to your students and planning your lessons on what you have heard and observed from them is key. One teacher recently shared her ongoing experiences of students utilizing different strategies for arriving at the same solution. She went on to share that when she allows her students the freedom of using their own strategies and methods of learning, they not only thrive, but are also much more enthusiastic about the subject matter.

Developing teaching strategies which allow students to utilize their own unique learning styles requires listening to how your students perceive their minds, bodies, and souls, and how they solve problems and complete assignments. It is a contradiction to expect students to be ready to listen and learn when they themselves are not being heard. As educators, let's not discourage our students' use of creativity in learning, but rather unleash it and allow it to thrive. Some students thrive more on the mind, others on the body, and others on the soul. A student who thrives on the mind is someone who easily engages with academic material; a student who thrives on the body is someone who needs team-building and physical activity to feel grounded and ready to learn; and a student who thrives on the soul is a student who needs to feel their story is heard before they can engage with academic material. A transformative educator learns to identify each of these types of students and provide them with the right resources to succeed.

The Pushouts documentary, which aired on the Public Broadcasting System (PBS) in 2019 and is available online at thepushouts.com, explores Victor's story from being a school "pushout" and gang member to a professor and author who works with educators to support at-promise students. As mentioned in an earlier chapter, Ms. Russ played a significant role in Victor's story, and helped him believe in himself by listening, offering encouragement, showing care, and treating him with dignity and respect. The film shows the authors of this book, Victor and Rebeca, leading a program for at-promise youth and teaching them strategies on how to build resiliency along with a team who can inspire and encourage them, while casting no judgments. Today, alongside their sociology and education students, they continue to mentor youths who have been pushed out by the school system.

ACTIVITY: APPLYING CULTURALLY RESPONSIVE TEACHING

The film "The Pushouts" can be used as a teaching tool for ways to be culturally responsive and effective in teaching at-promise students. For example, in one scene, we see a math teacher, Dr. Khadir Raja, who faced a challenge: how to teach complex mathematics to high school students who have persistently failed at the subject. With his unique, culturally relevant lesson plan, Dr. Raja presented algebraic expressions using popular culture and street vernacular. At the end of the day, even some of the least receptive students were solving complicated algebraic expressions. What are similar strategies you use to connect with students in your class? How can you replicate Dr. Raja's teaching method in your classroom?

CHAPTER 8

The Grocery Store Challenge: Providing Experiences for Students to Feel Happy

"Joy, feeling one's own value, being appreciated and loved by others, feeling useful and capable of production are all factors of enormous value for the human soul."

—MARIA MONTESSORI

THINK OF A GROCERY STORE where you received immaculate service. What are your reasons for choosing this specific place? How does this store make you feel every time you shop there?

In a study conducted by Forbes magazine, customers were asked questions similar to these to examine what makes top-ranked grocery stores so popular and successful. One in particular was continually ranked among the top five; it not only secures the highest rating in terms of the environment and fast checkouts, but also in having a staff who is kind and courteous—who constantly go above and beyond in responding to their customers' requests and needs. This particular grocery chain is Trader Joe's. It is known for surpassing customer expectations and satisfaction. Forbes names Trader Joe's' clients the "happiest customers in America." A key method for accomplishing this is through interacting and connecting with the customers. Trader Joe's values interactions with their customers, allowing them to receive high ratings on positive emotions because they strive to connect with their customers on an emotional level. They choose to not only ask if customers need assistance in locating certain items in the store, but also ask questions such as: "What are your plans this evening?" "Have you tried adding the masala sauce to your chicken?"

One day Victor walked into Trader Joe's at around 5pm after a long day of work. He was there to pick up groceries for the evening's family dinner. One item he purchased was a package of asparagus. Victor walked up to the register and the first thing the cashier said to him was, "Hello sir, how are you doing today?" Victor was not in the best mood and in a dragged-out voice, while staring at the ground, said, "I'm ok." The cashier looked at the asparagus and said, "Sir, what are you going to do with this asparagus?" Victor looked at the cashier with a smirk on his face and in a mean voice said, "I am going to cook it." The cashier replied, "Ok sir, when you get home grab a medium sauté pan, place olive oil in it, wait until the olive oil starts to create a white smoke --that is how you know it is ready-- toss the asparagus in the olive oil, add crushed sea salt and black pepper and stir for two minutes, just two minutes; you will have exquisite asparagus." By this time Victor had cheered up, had a smile on his face and thanked the cashier for the recipe. As Victor walked away he turned around and asked the cashier, "Hey man, don't you get tired of being nice to people all day long?" With a big smile on his face the cashier said, "No sir, because that is my job. To be nice to people." Then he pointed to the "bullpen" where the Trader Joe's managers where located and said, "And those guys are also very nice to me as well."

Trader Joe's courteous staff is constantly applauded for their awareness of their customers' needs, and they ensure that crewmembers are strolling through the aisles asking customers if they need anything, or just to smile and say a simple, "Hi."

What does this have to do with teachers and students, you may ask? Imagine an educational system where every educator sees it as their job to be nice to students all day long. This would radically alter our education system. And, what if administrators saw it as their job to treat their teachers and staff with cordiality and respect all day, everyday? This may have a deep impact in job satisfaction for teachers. The model Trader Joe's implements, which allows its customers to feel valued and known, is a model that educators should be utilizing in their classroom: always smile and be in tune with your students. Do your best to understand their needs and how to support them. Just as Trader Joe's' courteous staff is constantly on a quest to provide brilliant service, educators should be doing the same with their students—on an ongoing mission to know how to best support your students.

When asked to provide more positive support and cordial interactions to students, some educators will say, "I am not here to be their friend. I am here to teach them." In response we say, "It's ok. You don't have to be their friend, but please, please be friendly to them." Being friendly to students allows them to feel secure, safe, and cared for. A transformative teacher knows how to provide a cordial, caring experience to students and does not mind saying, "It is my job to be nice to students!"

ACTIVITY: THE TRADER JOE'S CHALLENGE

Directions: Share the teaching practices you have utilized which reflect the "Trader Joe's Challenge."

What do you value about good customer service as a customer?

How can some of these values be applied by educators?

What are some strategies for great "customer service" in educational settings?

What are some limitations and how can you get past them?

CHAPTER 9

"We Feel, Therefore We Learn": Implementing *an Emotion-Informed Approach to Teaching*

"I've learned that people will forget what you said, people will forget what you did, but people will never forget how you made them feel."

—MAYA ANGELOU

MANY MARGINALIZED YOUNG PEOPLE are misunderstood in educational settings and are often reprimanded, punished, harassed, or humiliated in an attempt to make them obedient, follow directions, and learn. Their creative responses to adversity can cause them to be singled out and admonished to "teach them a lesson." These students are viewed as problems to be fixed, rather than students with immense potential.

Punishment operates as a social fabric of everyday life for marginalized young people. This means that they are feeling treated as suspect on a daily basis, by various individuals in their community. These youth experience a kind of social death: they are considered outcasts before they even commit their first offense. For many of these students, school becomes a place where they feel disrespected, disciplined, and misunderstood rather than educated, and as a result, they develop an oppositional stance toward educational institutions and seek alternative spaces for acceptance and affirmation (Dance, 2002).

One reason why the educational system has failed to view young people as an asset is because many of those who work within this system have not been given adequate time and training to relate to this population and understand their struggles. Those teachers who know how to empathize and connect with students are often seen as "soft" by their colleagues. But what if we were to change the incentive system in education? What if we granted "extra prep time" (imagine what you would do with one or two less courses to teach per day) and "supplemental classroom funds" to educators who were identified by students as "caring?" This would allow teachers the resources and motivation to want to continue connecting with students. One of the obstacles to implementing this kind of policy in education is the assumption that implementing social-emotional practices in the classroom takes away from crucial academic time. However, research shows that when we teach the heart, the mind will follow. In other words, helping a student address emotional matters in the classroom is actually an investment in academic learning because the more grounded they feel, the more likely they are to learn academic material.

Neuroscientists Immordino, Yang, and Damasio (2007) conducted a study where they found that the part of the brain responsible for learning is intricately tied to the part of the brain responsible for emotion: "... learning, attention, memory, decision-making, and social functioning, are both profoundly affected by and subsumed within the processes of emotion..." (2007). Their study titled, "We feel, therefore we learn: The relevance of affective and social neuroscience to education" suggests that if educators want to improve their students' academic outcomes, they must first and foremost help their students work through emotional vulnerabilities. Emotions matter in teaching. Emotional states are associated with varying access to key parts of the brain required for learning. Negative emotional states—such as fear, anger and anxiety — have been linked to inhibition of the prefrontal cortex, or the "thinking" part of the brain. Because the frontal lobe, which is responsible for the function of reasoning, may not be fully developed until the age of 21 or 22, transformative teachers must adopt a developmental approach to teaching, being patient when students make mistakes, and are not able to empathize as much as an adult should.

In order to best connect and work with at-promise students, transformative educators must develop an ***emotion-informed approach*** to teaching. An emotion-informed approach encourages teachers to respond to their students with empathy and compassion in order to create a positive classroom environment that encourages space for connecting with students, being aware of their challenges, and not only seeing students' potential, but helping them believe it themselves. In addition, this approach allows the educator to understand the various types of support they can provide students. This creates the conditions for teachers to know what emotional support is and to utilize it on a daily basis.

According to researchers Woolley and Grogan-Kaylor (2006), "support from authority figures was the strongest predictor of school-appropriate behavior, positive attitudes toward school, and academic performance." Teachers are the authority figures whom students spend much of their time with; therefore, as an educator, it is important to know how to best support students. One strategy to use in understanding the "how" in supporting students is knowing the "what."

Researchers have detailed four types of teacher support:

1. INFORMATIONAL: "MY TEACHERS MAKE SURE I HAVE WHAT I NEED FOR SCHOOL."

Offering informational support includes providing students with the information, advice, suggestions, and resources necessary for students to succeed in their academics. For example, when teaching a new math lesson, a teacher who offers informational support would ensure their students have the necessary materials for the lesson, such as the appropriate type of calculator, lined paper for drawing graphs, etc.

2. **INSTRUMENTAL: "MY TEACHERS EXPLAIN THINGS I DON'T UNDERSTAND."**

   When teachers offer instrumental support, they are providing the type of aid required for their students to understand what they are being taught. For example, teachers may take extra time to explain the details of a lesson or assignment, even giving up their lunch break or staying longer after school to tutor their students.

3. **APPRAISAL: "MY TEACHERS TELL ME HOW WELL I DO ON TASKS."**

   Teachers who provide appraisal support offer their students information that is encouraging and serves as motivation for students' self-evaluation. Appraisal support can be given by reminding your students of all the qualities they possess that enable them to successfully pass a test or understand a new lesson.

4. **EMOTIONAL: "MY TEACHERS CARE ABOUT ME."**

   Demonstrating empathy, care, and trust are ways you can provide emotional support to your students. Many of your students may not receive this type of support elsewhere and may not even know how they can accept the care and kindness you offer to them.

Previous research has demonstrated that emotional support can significantly influence students' social skills and academic competence. Moreover, our research has shown that for low-income children, emotional support is needed more than informational support. In a survey we conducted on 1,879 high school students, the data demonstrated that emotional support made a larger impact than informational support for low-income students. In contrast, informational support had a larger impact than emotional support for students who come from a middle-class background. In other words, it may be the case that students from low-income backgrounds hanker for and thrive on emotional support more than students from middle-class backgrounds.

One way to offer emotional support to your students is to **express a genuine interest in your students' learning.** As a teacher, you should not only help your students with their schoolwork, but also listen to their ideas and feelings to demonstrate that you care for and respect them, and that you want them to fulfill their capabilities and potentialities, even if they each learn differently. Another way to offer emotional support is by providing **unconditional nurturing.** Allow students to feel that no matter how many mistakes they make, you are still going to nurture and care for them, because making mistakes is part of the process of learning and allows opportunities for growth and improvement.

Additionally, **showing consistency** is a way of offering emotional support. It is important to treat all of your students in the same manner. Differential treatment towards students can make them question themselves and why they are treated differently than their peers, potentially leading them to believe they are somehow less valued than other students.

Activity: Describe examples of each type of teacher support within the context of your classroom and subject area. Use the blank box for any other types of support you practice?

INFORMATIONAL SUPPORT	
INSTRUMENTAL SUPPORT	
APPRAISAL SUPPORT	
EMOTIONAL SUPPORT	

CHAPTER 10

Practical Recommendations for Connecting with Students and Addressing the Achievement Gap in Education

"Know about self, Know about your students,
Know about their families,
Know about their community!"
—SONIA NIETO

YOUR ROLE AS AN EDUCATOR makes a lasting impact on your students. Whether or not they realize it, their trajectory in school and life is directly related to the quality of interaction you provided them as their teacher. In order to support your students in their academic career, you must support them in their social-emotional development. Below are some guidelines to follow in your journey as a transformative teacher:

- It is important to first and foremost remember your purpose for entering into your teaching career. When you can remember your purpose for teaching, your "what" becomes more impactful to you and to the young people in your classroom.

- What type of lens do you see your students through: at-risk or at-promise? Let's change the way we perceive our students and focus on their immense capabilities and potentials, rather than on the things that may be challenging for them. When we use an at-promise rather than an at-risk perspective, we allow our students the support they need to thrive and grow in education.

- Making students feel seen and known can significantly impact their learning, because they will feel cared about as a whole person, rather than as a compilation of test scores and grades. Showing unconditional positive regard will give students the freedom to explore education without fear of being seen as "less than" when they don't ace a test or learn something quickly.

- Get to know your students. Where do they come from? What has their upbringing been like? What are their strengths and challenges? Don't let language become a "barrier"—human connection has no language!

- Emotions matter! Providing emotional support can influence students' social skills, academic competence, and even their educational outcomes. When students receive support from someone they trust, they will feel they are an asset to your classroom, allowing them to develop a sense of belonging, and they will consequently flourish.

- Let's value our students' stories. Educators should teach on the principle that stories of adversity and resilience are powerful. Help your students transform their narratives from ones of hardship to stories of strength and perseverance.

- Always be cordial, be in tune with your students, provide friendly interactions, and show genuine interest in their learning.

Understanding Racial and Cultural Literacy as an Educator

It is imperative for teachers to embrace the idea that students from low-income backgrounds are capable learners. Scholars note that it is significantly detrimental when teachers do not expect success from all of their students, and even believe that poverty decreases their likelihood of succeeding. Ladson-Billings (1994) argues that if students are treated as being capable, they will ultimately demonstrate that they are. This idea was reflected in our own research, when we conducted observations of one school and discovered a transformative teacher working to change their students' lives. One Latino student in the study was asked how he ended up in a particular class; he replied, "I was dragged in by Mrs. B." When we questioned why she "dragged him in," he responded "I guess she sees something in me." The majority of working-class students are highly capable and independent; some of these students will work tirelessly to meet their assignment deadlines, at times refusing free food from Mrs. B in order to complete their work. Mrs. B reported that one class was even caught breaking into school over the weekend to finish their projects. Mrs. B helped support and guide these students to incredible levels of success, eventually helping them place fourth in the statewide Business Plan competition in Bakersfield, California in 2017, in addition to receiving many other awards over the years. One of the Latino students was invited by the famous anthropologist Jane Goodall to a dinner because of his social entrepreneurship work on saving the jungle.

Best Practices in the Classroom

Based on a major four-year study we conducted at a high school with over 1800 students, where we collected survey data, interviews, observations, and held focus groups, we outline key ways in which teachers can help support students:

- A teacher can ask, how do I engage with my best students and how can I make this engagement universal with all students?

- Teachers must consistently demonstrate genuine emotional and instrumental support to students across race, gender, achievement, and class lines.

- Studies in cognitive sociology and psychology have shown that people are often unaware of the differential treatment that they engage in. One recommendation would be to have teachers videotape themselves teaching their various courses throughout the day. This provides them with rich data to measure differential treatment of students, and teachers can learn from these videos and adjust their practices accordingly.

- Teachers could begin the class with a daily check in, asking how students' weeks/weekends are going. This was observed in one classroom, where a distinct feeling of friendliness and emotional support has been cultivated. One Latina student commented to her teacher: "Your class is fun...your personality makes it fun." Further, this teacher demonstrated concern for the well-being of students by asking one white female student "You look sleepy. You alright?" He clapped hands with the student, "Get it together, girl." This teacher was one of the teachers identified by a random sample of students who were asked to name a "good teacher."

Another teacher also regularly engages with her students about their personal lives, as is seen in her interaction with a student one day in class. The teacher said to the student, "You can sit with me so we can talk." The student responds: "About what?" The teacher answers: "Life." This teacher also asked one of our researchers observing the class to put her in contact with someone who has resources for homeless adolescents, as one of her students and his mother had been living on the streets. During our observations, it became apparent that this teacher truly cares for her students. The teacher has sustained lasting relationships with her students. Many high school graduates return to her classroom to provide support to her current students, and some graduates who are attending the local community college return to her classroom to do their homework there.

- It is also important to support students' extracurricular activities and lives outside of the classroom. One teacher supported his student's achievement by announcing to his class that a fellow student is having an art show at a local gallery and encouraging all students to attend: "I would love it if we'd have a senior party at the gallery."

- Another science teacher who had two students on the soccer team supported them in giving a presentation that connected their sport to science. After the presentation, while the class was walking to another lab, the teacher asked the class to stop at the lawn and asked the team students to share some soccer moves. Everyone got in a circle as the students showed some fun soccer moves while everyone cheered and applauded.

- Classroom climate at the high school that was studied varied drastically from teacher to teacher, but more importantly from student-demographic to student-demographic. Teachers could work on improving their student-teacher interactions by keeping track of how many positive, cordial, supportive interactions they have with a diverse array of students throughout the day. Teachers could keep a journal while being trained. They could write down all the positive/negative/disinterested feelings they're having about students, and about the professional development program. Journals could be used to have real, constructive conversations with each other and with trainers or administrators.

- Teachers should discuss how they could embrace the following principal: "While college isn't for everyone, I believe that every student has the potential to attend college, and I am willing to consistently provide them the tools to do so." One teacher brought in an administrator to speak about the importance of passing an English exam. "If you take this and pass it, you're already ahead of the game. Don't blow it off." The teacher adds, "You pass this test, you're in college level English." To help them prepare for this exam, the teacher brought a college faculty member to administer a timed writing assignment. In addition to bringing in guest speakers to address college related topics, posters displaying SAT/ACT test dates and locations are posted on a classroom wall, as well as one displaying the average SAT/ACT scores at various universities. One teacher openly expresses to his students that a college degree is a reachable goal. He uses positive role models with similar upbringings who have graduated from a four-year university, as examples that earning a college degree is attainable.

- Provide students with a deeper and broader understanding of why their class subject matters.

- Increasing student engagement increases positive academic development. "Students are more likely to become engaged with authentic academic work that involves them in a process of meaningful inquiry to solve real life problems that extend beyond the classroom" (Abi-Nader, 2011, p. 159). "Centering learning process on children's actual experiences, relating what students learn to matters of personal interest, linking classroom learning to relevant events and experiences in student's lives, tying what is learned to the community or the larger society, and drawing connections across topics and subjects—can bring about better learning outcomes" (Boykin & Noguera, 2011). We found that teachers who were labeled as "cool" and "supportive" by low-income students were teachers that centered learning around life experiences, across academic subjects. During one lunch period, a research assistant randomly asked several students who they thought were "good teachers." A Latino and a Latina separately mentioned the same teacher. "Mr. Johnson is unlike other teachers. He helps with actual life." During that same lunch period, students also identified teachers whom we had observed as providing emotional support to their students during class. These teachers were witnessed frequently asking their students about what is going on with them outside of the classroom.

- Incorporate culturally-relevant pedagogy in the classroom. One teacher in our study was observed providing a culturally-relevant approach to his students. During his lectures, he frequently integrated the topic of race into class discussion and curriculum. These discussions helped students engage in critical thinking. Additionally, before class he played music that the students either recognized or were interested in learning about, such as reggae, hip hop, and R&B. This use of familiar music may have served as a form of emotional support. Additionally, it is important to note that his decision to play certain genres of music was genuine —This teacher played it because he also liked these genres of music. We also witnessed other teachers develop close relationships with their students by being aware of and supporting their students' life experiences.

- Help students apply the information they learn in school to real-life situations. One teacher helps his students understand how the lessons they're learning in school can be applied to their lives outside of school. By working through algebra, the teacher explains that he is training their brain to, "work in a logical, common sense, step-by-step way." The teacher emphasized to his students the importance of improving these skills for a future job and everyday life. He then asked the class, "Now, tell me, when will you use algebra in real life?" One student responded: "Maybe if you're working as a cashier at a register." The teacher responds: "That's a good example, it shows us that it's hard to live without math."

ACTIVITY: PROMOTING EMOTION-INFORMED APPROACHES

List steps that you can to promote an emotion-informed approach in your classroom

APPENDIX

Research Supporting Emotion-Informed Approaches

(WITH SHADI ROSHANDEL)

"My contention is, first, that we should want more from our educational efforts than adequate academic achievement and, second, that we will not achieve even that meager success unless our children believe that they themselves are cared for and learn to care for others."

—NEL NODDINGS

SCHOOLS PLAY AN INCREASINGLY IMPORTANT ROLE during early adolescence, not only because youth spend a significant amount of time in the classroom, but also because teachers and schools have the opportunity to provide students with resources and options concerning their futures that they may not receive otherwise (Anderman, Anderman, & Griesinger, 1999). Possible selves represent a person's belief about what they might be like in the future (Markus & Nurius, 1968). School-relevant resources may be instrumental in helping students develop possible selves in academic and career domains, and secondary school teachers have a great deal of control over such resources. Furthermore, possible selves are particularly sensitive to situations that can communicate new and inconsistent information about themselves (Markus & Nurius, 1986). As teachers expose adolescents to novel and unique information, possible selves may be vulnerable to this new knowledge. Therefore, teachers can be influential in developing adolescents' possible selves, as they may provide options that the adolescents never thought possible.

Perceived Teacher Support

Teachers can be important supportive figures in an adolescent's life. Research consistently finds the relationship between teachers and students to be one of the most important factors in students' success (Wentzel, 1997; 1998). Interview data from 28 primarily African American and Latino first-year college students revealed that two participants mentioned their teachers as a significant influence for them to consider going to college as part of their educational possible selves. Both adolescents mentioned that they started considering college attendance because their teachers provided them with resources on how to qualify for and attend college, as well as with the encouragement to believe that college was a possibility (Pizzolato, 2006). Although this study highlights in the influence of teachers on developing adolescents' hoped-for and expected possible selves, this was not the main focus of the study; the data emerged through the interviews.

Adolescent Self-Concept and Possible Selves

There is also evidence that adolescents perceive teachers as a source of support, and these perceptions influence psychological constructs that are similar to possible selves, such as the self-concept. The term self-concept is defined as a person's beliefs about himself or herself and who they are (Baumeister, 1999). Within classroom contexts, teachers can promote opportunities for students to reflect on their future educational goals and aspirations. Teachers are in a unique position to support adolescents' hopes and dreams for the future and help them to understand the impact of their school performance on their educational possible selves and self-concept (Day, Borkowski, Punzo, & Howsepian, 1994). Brewster and Bowen (2004) also found that Latina/o adolescents' positive school engagement was associated with perceptions of their teachers as encouraging.

Teacher support has been found to have significant implications for adolescents' self-concept and aspirations for the future. In an ethnically diverse sample of adolescents ages 9-16, Benner and Mistry (2007) used secondary analysis of data from an antipoverty program targeting low income neighborhoods in order to examine the effects of teacher expectations on adolescent achievement outcomes, including influencing one's self-concept of their ability to go to college. Results indicated that *teachers' expectations of college attendance correlated positively with adolescents' self-concept*. Similarly, in a sample of predominantly low-income high school students of color, Felner and colleagues (Felner, Aber, Primavera, & Cauce, 1985) found that perceived teacher support was positively correlated with participants' self-concept, measured by a summary score of scholastics, peer and family relationships, and general self-concept measures.

Demaray and colleagues (2009) examined the relationship between perceived availability of teacher support and children's self-concept in a sample of primarily white students in grades 3-12. Data were collected using the Child and Adolescent Social Support Scale (CASSS), which assesses perceptions of social support from parents, teachers, classmates, and close friends. In addition, the Student Self-Concept Scale (SSCS) was used to measure global self-concept. Global self-concept scores were found to be significantly and positively related to both perceived teacher support and ratings of the importance of teacher support. These studies together demonstrate that perceived teacher support relates to students' self-concepts. Given that the construct of possible selves is a component of the self-concept, given that possible selves are mental representations of the self in the future, it is reasonable to expect a relationship between perceived teacher support and adolescents' possible selves. However, further research is necessary to examine the role teachers play in developing and supporting adolescents' possible selves.

Academic Outcomes and Perceived Teacher Support

Researchers have also explored the relationship between perceived teacher support and educational outcomes, such as academic engagement, effort, expectations, motivation, and achievement. Wentzel (1997) studied a group of Caucasian adolescents' perceptions of teacher support in relation to their motivation to achieve positive social and academic outcomes in middle school. Perceived teacher support was measured by the Teacher Social and Academic Support subscales of the Classroom Life Measure and related to both behavioral and affective engagement. Behavioral engagement was defined as what students do to remain involved in learning (Hudley & Daoud, 2008), and affective engagement included attitudes or feelings about the pursuit of learning (Skinner & Belmont, 1993). Results showed that teacher support positively and significantly correlated with GPA and academic effort. In a similar sample of junior high students, Midgley, Feldlaufer, and Eccles (1989) wanted to determine if changes in students' perceptions of student/teacher relationships during the transition to junior high school influenced their valuing of mathematics. *The study of 1301 students indicated that students who perceived their teachers to be highly supportive valued math, while students who perceived teachers to be low in support suffered a steady decline in their valuing of math.* These studies together support the significant impact perceived teacher support has on adolescents' academic engagement and motivation, and, overall, their academic outcomes.

Significance of Teacher Support on Academic Outcomes.
Although many adolescents perceive their parents and peers to be greater sources of support than teachers (Wentzel, 1997), some social support literature has found that academic outcomes are most strongly influenced by perceived teacher support compared to support from other entities in students' lives. Wentzel (1998) found that when perceived support from parents, teachers, and peers was considered simultaneously, teacher support had a direct relationship with academic outcomes, whereas both parental support and peer support were associated with academic outcomes only indirectly through students' emotional well being. Chen (2005) similarly explored the relationship between perceived teacher, parent, and peer support and academic engagement amongst a group of 270 adolescents in a Hong Kong secondary school. Perceived teacher support positively correlated with self-reported academic engagement and grades in English, Chinese, and math classes. However, while perceived teacher support was positively related to academic achievement, perceived parental support was negatively related to achievement.

In addition, in a recent study of 226 Latino youth from an urban middle school, Garcia-Reid, Reid, & Peterson (2005) reported that *teacher support had the highest impact on school engagement in a model that included measures of support from parents, friends, and neighborhood adults*. Similarly, based on a sample of 9th and 10th grade Latino/a youth, *teacher academic support was the only variable associated with increased academic motivation for both boys and girls* (Alfaro, Umaña-Taylor, & Bámaca, 2006). Finally, in a diverse sample of middle and high school students, Woolley and Grogan-Kaylor (2006) found *teacher support to be the strongest predictor of school-appropriate behavior, positive attitudes toward school, and academic performance*. None of these studies specified the type of teacher support associated with academic outcomes, as a composite score was created and included multiple, distinct types of support. It is therefore difficult to distinguish which types of support were salient. The literature reviewed here suggests that teacher support is influential in an array of academic and behavioral domains and that teachers are in a unique position to help their students understand the benefits of school success on educational possible selves (Day et al., 1994).

Individual Differences in Perceived Teacher Support

Gender Differences.

Although perceived teacher support is associated with engagement for both boys and girls, the relationship differs by gender. For example, Goodenow (1993) investigated the association between perceived teacher support and motivation in 353 middle school students who were primarily white and of European-American ancestry, using an expectancy-value framework. Results indicated that teacher support explained over one-third of students' interest, perceived importance of the academic subject, and value of their class, suggesting that academic motivation may be influenced by perceived teacher support. However, teacher support demonstrated stronger relationships with motivational variables for girls than for boys. While girls' and boys' expectations for success and valuing of academic learning did not differ, girls' expectations and valuing of academic learning were found to be positively related to perceptions of good relationships with teachers.

Wilson & Wilson (1992) also examined the relationship between perceived teacher support and adolescents' future aspirations in a large sample of majority white high school seniors, and found gender differences within their results. Adolescents' future aspirations were measured by asking participants, "What is the lowest level of education you would be satisfied with?" and explored perceived teacher support by asking adolescents two questions: "What do your teachers think you ought to do after high school?" and "How much have your teachers influenced your high school program?" Results indicated that adolescents who perceived high teacher support for their aspirations were more likely to have higher aspirations than adolescents who perceived low teacher support for their aspirations. These results again differed across gender, as female aspirations were more strongly influenced by perceived teacher support than those of males.

Similarly, Green and colleagues (Green, Rhodes, Hirsch, Suárez-Orozco, & Camic, 2008) explored the relationship between perceived teacher support and academic engagement among 139 immigrant students born in Mexico and Central America in grades 4 through 8. Using HLM analysis, *perceptions of support were positively related to youths' academic engagement*, and results differentially predicted engagement trajectories, depending on gender. For girls, higher levels of support predicted higher initial engagement, whereas for boys, support had no effect on initial engagement, but predicted positive changes in engagement over time.

Ethnic Differences.

In addition to gender differences, researchers have also found ethnic differences in how students respond to perceived support from their teachers. Hudley,Daoud, Polanco, Wright-Castro, and Hershberg (2003) examined the relationship between perceived teacher support, engagement, and adolescents' educational expectations within a group of 190 high school students, from a balanced Latino and white population. Teacher support was defined as both emotional warmth ("This teacher really cares about us"), and academic validation ("My teacher thinks I am a good student"). Future expectations were measured by two questions: "If you could do anything you wanted when you graduate, how possible is it that you will go to a four-year college or university?" and "If you could do anything you wanted, how possible is it that you will have a professional job that requires college training?"

Results indicated that perceived teacher support was the only significant predictor of all measures of engagement, which included GPA, discipline records, and self-reported affective engagement (attitudes toward achievement). In addition, both college and career expectations were significantly related to teacher-reported behavioral and affective engagement. Perceived teacher support marginally predicted college expectations for all students, and also predicted engagement, which in turn predicted expectations. However, the groups differed in important ways. For Latinos, teacher warmth was more important, and for whites, academic validation was more important in relationship to students' affective engagement. Furthermore, higher achieving Latinos who enjoyed school had higher future expectations, but lower achieving Latinos had lower career expectations, irrespective of whether they enjoyed school. However, both high and low achieving white students had higher future expectations if they enjoyed school. Together these studies suggest that perceived teacher support is particularly relevant to adolescents' educational goals; however, it is essential to consider differences by gender and ethnicity.

Types of Perceived Teacher Support

A limited number of studies exploring perceived teacher support have focused on the relationship between specific types of support and adolescent outcomes. For the purpose of this book, perceived teacher support has been operationalized as four types of support (House, 1981; Tardy, 1985): emotional support (e.g., teachers show "care" for students), instrumental support (e.g., teachers explain things that students don't understand), informational support (e.g., teachers make sure students have what they need for school), and appraisal support (e.g., teachers tell students how well they do on tasks). Despite the recognition of these different types of support, many studies have focused on global measures of perceived support and do not examine specific types of support. These more fine-grained definitions may have the detail to provide further insights into perceived social support more generally, however, the few studies that do focus on the specific type of perceived teacher support are mixed (Malecki & Demaray, 2003).

For example, in an ethnically diverse sample of adolescents in grades 5 through 8, Malecki and Demaray (2003) examined the types of support children most often perceive from their teachers. Students perceived teacher informational support to be significantly more frequent than teachers' emotional, appraisal, and instrumental support. Moreover, teacher appraisal support was perceived significantly more frequently than instrumental support. However, no meaningful gender differences were found. The results from this study indicate that both boys and girls perceive informational support from teachers more often than emotional support. However, student perceptions of emotional support from teachers were the only significant individual predictor of teacher ratings of academic competence. These results suggest that teachers should be aware of the type of support they are providing their students and find a balance between these different types of support, because they can all be consequential and meaningful.

A cross-cultural study examined types of perceived teacher support amongst adolescents living in the U.S. and Finland (Davidson, Demaray, Malecki, Ellonen, & Korkiamaki, 2008). The sample included 148 adolescents from a Midwestern high school and 144 adolescents from a variety of Finnish schools. Using the CASSS, their findings revealed that participants from the U.S. perceived higher levels of total support, as well as higher levels of each type of social support, as compared to Finnish participants. Instrumental support demonstrated the greatest difference between the two groups. The researchers speculate that Finnish students more often obtain this type of support from formal governmental institutions rather than teachers (Davidson et al., 2008).

Similarly, Suldo and colleagues (Suldo, Friedrich, White, Farmer, Minch, & Michalowski, 2009) conducted a mixed-methods study to identify which types of perceived teacher support are most strongly associated with middle school students' well being. Survey data from 401 adolescents indicated that perceived teacher support accounted for 16 percent of variance in all students' well-being, with emotional and instrumental support uniquely predicting student well-being. These results did not differ by gender, however, qualitative data collected from a subset of 50 adolescents revealed gender differences in the specific actions and/or comments teachers use to communicate their support. Girls commented more on interpersonal interactions, such as teachers' influences on their emotional states, whereas boys focused on achievement, such as how teachers helped them improve their grades. Collectively, these studies, although few, suggest that researchers examining perceived teacher support amongst adolescents need to look at the specific types of support and their relationships with educational outcomes, while also considering possible gender and ethnic differences.

Culturally Relevant Programs

There is a greater opportunity for equitable schools when classrooms are "responsive to the social and cultural diversity of the communities that they serve" (Cairney, 2000, p.10). Researcher Jim Cummins "identified four structural elements of schooling, which," he argued, "influence the extent to which students from minority backgrounds are empowered or disadvantaged." The following elements include incorporating minority students' cultures and languages, including minority communities in the education of their children, pedagogical assumptions and practices operating in the classroom, and the assessment of minority students" (Cairney, 2000, p. 6).

- *Culturally responsive teaching* recognizes certain cultural features of Latinos and incorporates those aspects into the curriculum (Waxman & Pardon, 2002). For example, a teacher who understands that Latinos place great importance on family and community would incorporate those aspects into their lessons, (Waxman & Pardon, 2002). Teachers can also create a cooperative learning environment where students work in small groups, which has been found to decrease student anxiety and improve English proficiency and social, academic, and communication skills (Calderon, 1991; Christian, 1995; Rivera & Zehler, 1991). Also, teachers who provide opportunities for extended dialogue are especially effective in teaching Latino students, because these practices will help such students develop language skills and higher-level thinking skills (Duran, Dugan, & Weffer, 1997; Hakuta & August, 1998; Tharp, 1995). Another benefit of using culturally relevant pedagogy is that students are less likely to experience the effects of discrimination they may experience (Taylor, 2007).

- Dr. Carol Dweck found that by moving students into a "growth mindset," in which students recognize that they can make their minds grow and constantly improve their abilities, these students increased their engagement levels (Blackwell, Trzesniewski, & Dweck, 2007), improved their math and verbal test scores, narrowed the math gender gap for girls, and increased the GPA for Latino middle school students at a California middle school (Good, Aronson, & Inzlicht, 2003). There are three programs: Mindset Works School Kit, Brainology for students, which combines online instruction with 10 hours of classroom activities, and a professional-development program for teachers, which includes five online modules. We recommend that schools look into these kinds of professional development.

- Career Academies prepare students for both college and careers by weaving a particular career theme throughout the academy and coursework. Students are admitted into the academies, and each academy enrolls between 100 to 300 students. Teachers in the academy work together to integrate career themes into their lessons, and local businesses related to the particular career are connected to the academy and provide internships to 11th and 12th graders. Career Academies have been found to improve attendance, increase credit accumulation, and increase graduation rates for students enrolled in the academies (Jossey-Bass, 1992; McPartland, Balfanz, Jordan, & Legters, 1998).

- One of the most influential books on the topic of closing the achievement gap is *Why Race and Culture Matter in Schools: Closing the Achievement Gap in America's Classrooms* by Tyrone C. Howard (2010). Below we summarize his recommendations based on extensive research:
  - » Any attempt to construct a knowledge base for classroom teachers should recognize important racial roles and teaching with "a cultural eye" (Irvine, 2003). Having a cultural eye in teaching refers to when "teachers view their world and the work that they do through a cultural lens that allows them to be change agents in the academic performance of culturally diverse students" (Irvine, 2003)
  - » Teachers must find a realistic, positive idea of where and how students can grow socially and academically. They must also understand the roles that poverty, class, race, etc. play in society and education.
  - » Some teachers are sympathetic educators who "water down" curriculum because they see limitations in students' abilities to learn and view learning as teacher-dominate. On the other

hand, empathetic teachers understand their students' circumstances, yet see promise and possibilities in students and view learning as a reciprocal process between teacher and student. Empathetic teaching is effective because it sets all students to the same standards and levels of reason for lower educational outcomes for students from culturally diverse backgrounds.

» Culturally responsive pedagogy recognizes the uniqueness of student culture, teaches "to and through the strengths" of students, and is culturally "validating and affirming."
» Caring is a key element in a teacher's ability to empower students, as well as to see themselves as transformative agents.
» Some researchers believe that effective teaching should recognize the complexities of teaching and the need for teachers to develop breadth and depth of pedagogy, content, and students' backgrounds to enhance learning.

Developing Cultural Competence and Racial Awareness in Classroom Teachers

By developing a better understanding of race and culture and their roles in school settings, educators can take steps to relieve the achievement gaps in educational outcomes between African American, Native American, and Latino students. Cultural competence is "a set of behaviors, attitudes, and policies that come together in a system or agency, or among professionals, to allow for effective work in cross-cultural situations." This framework is offered by the National Center for Cultural Competence: http://nccc.georgetown.edu/resources/assessments.html.

- Examining cultural competence helps educators realize whether they hold deficit-based notions, distorted views, or negative perceptions of culturally diverse students, low-income communities, and students' families.

- Teachers must be open-minded in adjusting their preconceptions about marginalized groups because it is difficult to realize that our beliefs are incorrect.

- Culturally competent educators must have racial awareness of the role of race in U.S. society and whiteness—"Racial awareness is the willingness of educators to listen to students talk about their racialized experiences, to probe for deeper clarity about these experiences, and to seek ways to learn from them."

- Cultural competence in the classroom allows students to engage in readings and activities that pertain to their racial identities.

- Teachers must delve into race-related topics because many don't have experiential knowledge regarding issues of race; it becomes easy to practice "colorblindness."

In other studies, African American and Latino students identified teacher encouragement as a motive for their effort, and substantially indicated that this encouragement was more motivating than teacher demands, unlike white students, who cited demands more than their minority peers as motivating their academic efforts. But white students also indicated that teacher encouragement was an incentive for them to make an effort to achieve. Therefore, it is important for schools to continue to identify the practices that are effective and to create a systematic plan for expanding these practices and improving the way that at-promise students are educated and supported. A transformative teacher who takes the time and has the courage to have serious discussions about emotional intelligence, race, class, culture, equity, teaching strategies, and self-reflection will build a stronger, more equitable, empathic learning community rendering all students at-promise!

References

Abi-Nader, J., 2011. A house for my mother: Motivating Hispanic high school students. *Anthropology & Education Quarterly, 1*(21), 41-58.

Alfaro, E. C., Umaña Taylor, A. J., & Bámaca, M. Y. (2006). The influence of academic support on Latino adolescents' academic motivation. *Family Relations, 55*(3), 279-291.

Anderman, E. M., Anderman, L. H., & Griesinger, T. (1999). The relation of present and possible academic selves during early adolescence to grade point average and achievement goals. *The Elementary School Journal, 100*(1), 3-17.

Anderson, A. R., Christenson, S. L., Sinclair, M. F., & Lehr, C. A. (2004). Check and connect: the importance of relationships for promoting engagement with school. *Journal of School Psychology, 42*, 95-113.

Aspiazu, G. G., Bauer, S. C., & Spillett, M. D. (1998). Improving the academic performance of Hispanic youth: A community education model. Bilingual Research Journal, 22(2), 1-20.

Baumeister, R. F. (1999). Self-concept, self-esteem, and identity. In V. Derlega, B. Winstead, & W. Jones (Eds.), Personality: Contemporary Theory and Research 2nd ed. (pp. 339–375). Chicago, IL: Nelson-Hall.

Benner, A. D., & Mistry, R. S. (2007). Congruence of mother and teacher educational expectations and low-income youth's academic competence. Journal of Educational Psychology, 99(1), 140-153.

Benson, J. (2016). The power of positive regard. Educational Leadership, 73(9), 22-26.

Blackwell, L.S., Trzesniewski, K.H., & Dweck, C.S. (2007). Implicit theories of intelligence predict achievement across an adolescent transition: A longitudinal study and an intervention. Child Development, 78, 246-263.

Boykin, A. W., & Noguera, P. (2011). Creating the opportunity to learn: Moving from research to practice to close the achievement gap. Ascd.

Brewster, A. B., & Bowen, G. L. (2004). Teacher support and the school engagement of Latino middle and high school students at risk of school failure. Child and Adolescent Social Work Journal, 21(1), 47-67.

Cabrera, A. F., Deil-Amen, R., Prabhu, R., Terenzini, P. T., Lee, C., & Franklin, Jr, R. E. (2006). Increasing the college preparedness of at-risk students. Journal of Latinos and Education, 5(2), 79

Cairney, T. H. (2000). Beyond the classroom walls: The rediscovery of the family and community as partners in education. Educational Review, 52(2), 163-174.

Calderon, M. (1991). Benefits of cooperative learning for Hispanic students. Texas Research Journal, 2, 39-57.

Chen, J. J. L. (2005). Relation of academic support from parents, teachers, and peers to Hong Kong adolescents' academic achievement: The mediating role of academic engagement. Genetic, Social, and General Psychology Monographs, 131(2), 77-127.

Christian, D. (1995). Two-way bilingual education. Teaching Linguistically and Culturally Diverse Learners: Effective Programs and Practices. Santa Cruz, CA: National Center for Research on Cultural Diversity and Second Language Learning, pp. 8-11.

Comer, J. P. (2005). Child and adolescent development: The critical missing focus in school reform. Phi Delta Kappan, 86(10), 757-763.

Crenshaw, K. (1989). Demarginalizing the intersection of race and sex: A Black feminist critique of antidiscrimination doctrine, feminist theory and antiracist politics. In University of Chicago Legal Forum. Vol. 140, p. 139.

Davidson, L. M., Demaray, M. K., Malecki, C. K., Ellonen, N., & Korkiamäki, R. (2008). United States and Finnish adolescents' perceptions of social support: A cross-cultural analysis. School Psychology International, 29(3), 363-375.

Day, J. D., Borkowski, J. G., Punzo, D., & Howsepian, B. (1994). Enhancing possible selves in Mexican American students. Motivation and Emotion, 18(1), 79-103.

Decker, L. E., & Decker, V. (2003). Home, school, and community partnerships. Lanham, MD: Scarecrow Press.

Delgado-Gaitan, C. (2001). The power of community: Mobilizing for family and community. Boulder, CO: Rowman & Littlefield.

Demaray, M. K., Malecki, C. K., Rueger, S. Y., Brown, S. E., & Summers, K. H. (2009). The role of youth's ratings of the importance of socially supportive behaviors in the relationship between social support and self-concept. Journal of Youth and Adolescence, 38(1), 13-28. doi:10.1007/s10964-007-9258-3

Duran, B., Dugan, T., & Weffer, R. (1997). Increasing teacher effectiveness with language minority students. The High School Journal, 84, 238-246.

Fashola, S., & Slavin, R. (1998). Effective Dropout Prevention and College Attendance Programs for Students Placed at Risk, Journal of Education for Students Placed at Risk, 3(2), 159-183

Felner, R. D., Aber, M. S., Primavera, J., & Cauce, A. M. (1985). Adaptation and vulnerability in high-risk adolescents: An examination of environmental mediators. American Journal of Community Psychology, 13, 365-379.

Gándara, P. (2002). A study of high school Puente: What we have learned about preparing Latino youth for postsecondary education. Educational Policy, 16 (4), 474-495. DOI: 10.1177/0895904802164002

Gándara P., & Moreno, J. F. (2002). Introduction: The Puente Project: Issues and perspectives on preparing Latino youth for higher education. Educational Policy, 16(4), 463-473.

Garcia-Reid, P., Reid, R. J., & Peterson, N. A. (2005). School engagement among Latino youth in an urban middle school context: Valuing the role of social support. Education and Urban Society, 37(3), 257-275.

Gonzalez, M. C. (1995). Like mother like daughter: Intergenerational programs for Hispanic girls. Educational Considerations, 22(2), 17-30.

Good, C., Aronson, J., & Inzlicht, M. (2003). Improving adolescents' standardized test performance: An intervention to reduce the effects of stereotype threat. Applied Developmental Psychology, 24, 645-662.

Goodenow, C. (1993). Classroom belonging among early adolescent students: Relationships to motivation and achievement. The Journal of Early Adolescence, 13(1), 21-43.

Green, G., Rhodes, J., Hirsch, A. H., Suárez-Orozco, C., & Camic, P. M. (2008). Supportive adult relationships and the academic engagement of Latin American immigrant youth. Journal of School Psychology, 46(4), 393-412.

Hakuta, K., & August, D. (1998). Educating language-minority children. Washington, DC: National Academy Press

Haberman, M. (1995). Star teachers of children in poverty. West Lafayette, IN: Kappa Delta Pi.

Howard, T. C. (2010). Why race and culture matter in schools: Closing the achievement gap in America's classrooms (Vol. 39). Teachers College Press.

Hudley, C., & Daoud, A. M. (2008). Cultures in contrast: Understanding the influence of school culture on student engagement. In C. Hudley and A. E. Gottfried (Eds.), Academic Motivation and the Culture of School in Childhood and Adolescence (pp. 187-217). New York, NY: Oxford University Press.

Hudley, C., Daoud, A., Polanco, T., Wright-Castro, R., & Hershberg, R. (2003). Student engagement, school climate, and future expectations in high school.

Irvine, J. J. (2003). Educating teachers for diversity: Seeing with a cultural eye (Vol. 15). Teachers College Press.

Ladson-Billings, G. (1994). The dreamkeepers: Successful teachers of African American children. San Francisco, CA: Jossey-Bass.

Larson, K. A. & Rumberger, R. W. (1995). ALAS: Achievement for Latinos through academic success. In H. Thorton (Ed.), Staying in school: A technical report of three dropout prevention projects for middle school students with learning and emotional disabilities (pp. A-1—A-71). Minneapolis, MN: University of Minnesota, Institute on Community Integration.

Malecki, C. K., & Demaray, M. K. (2003). What Type of Support Do They Need? Investigating Student Adjustment as Related to Emotional, Informational, Appraisal, and Instrumental Support. School Psychology Quarterly, 18(3), 231-252.

Markus, H., & Nurius, P. (1986). Possible selves. American Psychologist, 41(9), 954-969.

McLeod, S. (2014). Carl Rogers. Retrieved from: https://www.simplypsychology.org/carl-rogers.html

McPartland, J., Balfanz, R., Jordan, W., & Legters, N. (1998). Improving climate and achievement in a troubled urban high school through the Talent Development Model. Journal of Education for Students Placed at Risk, 3(4), 337-361.

Midgley, C., Feldlaufer, H., & Eccles, J. S. (1989). Student/teacher relations and attitudes toward mathematics before and after the transition to junior high school. Child Development, 981-992.

Pizzolato, J. E. (2006). Achieving college student possible selves: Navigating the space between commitment and achievement of long-term identity goals. Cultural Diversity and Ethnic Minority Psychology, 12(1), 57-69.

Rivera, C., & Zehler, A. M. (1991). Assuring the academic success of language minority students: Collaboration in teaching and learning. Journal of Education, 173(2), 52-77.

Skinner, E. A., & Belmont, M. J. (1993). Motivation in the classroom: Reciprocal effects of teacher behavior and student engagement across the school year. Journal of Educational Psychology, 85(4), 571-581.

Suldo, S. M., Friedrich, A. A., White, T., Farmer, J., Minch, D., & Michalowski, J. (2009). Teacher support and adolescents' subjective well-being: A mixed-methods investigation. School Psychology Review, 38(1), 67-85.

Tardy, C. H. (1985). Social support measurement. American Journal of Community Psychology, 13(2), 187-202.

Tharp, R. G. (1995). Instructional conversations in Zuni classrooms. Teaching Linguistically and Culturally Diverse Learners: Effective Programs and Practices. Santa Cruz, CA: National Center for Research on Cultural Diversity and Second Language Learning, pp. 12-13.

Valenzuela, A. (2010). Subtractive schooling: US-Mexican youth and the politics of caring. Suny Press.

Waxman, H. C., & Pardon, Y. N. (2002). Research-based teaching practices that improve the education of English language learners. In L. Minaya-Rowe (Ed.),Teacher Training and Effective Pedagogy in the Context of Student Diversity (pp. 3-38). Greenwich, CT: Information Age.

Wentzel, K. R. (1997). Student motivation in middle school: The role of perceived pedagogical caring. Journal of Educational Psychology, 89(3), 411-419.

Wentzel, K. R. (1998). Social relationships and motivation in middle school: The role of parents, teachers, and peers. Journal of Educational Psychology, 90(2), 202-209.

Wilson, P. M., & Wilson, J. R. (1992). Environmental influences on adolescent educational aspirations: A logistic transform model. Youth & Society, 24(1), 52-70.

Woolley, M. E., & Grogan-Kaylor, A. (2006). Protective family factors in the context of neighborhood: Promoting positive school outcomes. Family Relations, 55(1), 93-104.

Made in the USA
Las Vegas, NV
15 September 2021